Georg Kugler

ELISABETH

Empress of Austria - Queen of Hungary

BONECHI VERLAG STYRIA

CONTENTS

Distributor for Austria
VERLAG STYRIA
Schönaugasse 64
A-8010 GRAZ

for Germany
Butzon & Bercker GmbH
Hooge Weg 71
D-47623 Kevelaer

for Switzerland
Herder AG Basel
Muttenzerstraße 109
CH-4133 Pratteln 1

Original title:
ELISABETH Kaiserin von Österreich - Königin von Ungarn

Concept and design: Casa Editrice Bonechi
Coordination: Monica Bonechi
Design, layout and cover: Sonia Gottardo
Page makeup: Laura Settesoldi
Editing: Giovannella Masini
English translation: Anthony Brierley

Text: Georg Kugler

Via Cairoli 18/b I-50131 Firenze
E-mail: bonechi@bonechi.it - Internet: www.bonechi.it

Printed in Italy by Centro Stampa Editoriale Bonechi

INDEX OF ILLUSTRATIONS

Graphische Sammlung Albertina, Vienna *(page 23)*; Archiv für Kunst und Geschichte, Berlin *(page 27 right)*; Bildarchiv der Österreichischen Nationalbibliothek *(pages 1, 9, 11 below, 12 above, 14 above, 15 below, 17, 21 below, 24, 26 left, 27 left, 28, 31, 34, 36 above, 37 below, 38, 41, 43 below, 44, 45, 47, 50, 51, 53)*; Bundesmobiliendepot Vienna *(pages 7, 35, 37 above and centre, 46, 56 left, 59 left, 60/61)*; Historisches Museum der Stadt Vienna *(pages 18 below, 21 above, 42, 43 above, 48, 49, 56 right)*; Hotel Beau-Rivage, Geneva *(page 58 below)*; Dr. Hans Kräftner, Vienna *(page 57)*; Kunsthandlung Haßfurther, Vienna *(page 15* above*)*; Kunsthistorisches Museum Vienna *(pages 10, 11 above, 12 below, 13, 14 below, 16, 18/19, 19 below, 20, 22, 25, 29, 30, 32, 36 below, 39, 40, 52, 54)*; Residenz-Galerie Salzburg *(Photo Ulrich Ghezzi: page 26 right)*; Schloß Schönbrunn Kultur- und Betriebs-Gesellschaft *(pages 62, 63)*; Stadtmuseum Munich *(pages 4, 5, 8)*; Ungarisches Nationalmuseum, Budapest *(pages 55, 58 above)*.
All the other originals come from the archives of Styria publishers and Bonechi.

ISBN 3 - 222 - 12660 - 7

CHILDHOOD AND YOUTH IN BAVARIA

The splendour and tragic aura surrounding this fascinating yet strangely contradictory woman, notwithstanding or perhaps because of her elevated social and political position as empress and queen of a great European empire, have had a lasting and deeply-felt effect up until the present day, making Elisabeth a cult figure of our times. It was not a preordained destiny; it was not marked out for her by her parents. Elisabeth was born on Christmas Eve 1837 in Munich, a princess "in Bavaria", not the daughter of a king "of Bavaria" of the house of Wittelsbach but rather the daughter of duke Maximilian, of the line of the counts palatine of Birkenwald-Gelnhausen in the Rhineland Palatinate. Her grandfather on her father's side, William, had married a sister of the crown prince and future king Maximilian Joseph of Bavaria, from whom he had been conferred the title of duke "in Bavaria", a title lacking any real political influence. Elisabeth's family was therefore related to the royal family of Bavaria, and Elisabeth's mother, Ludovica, was also a Wittelsbach. Relations with the royal family were therefore close, and Munich and its court were the hub of social life. With the reign of king Ludwig I (1825-1848), the city had entered its true classical age. Thanks to royal patronage and public building, it had assumed a status among the leading German residences, was considered a capital of the arts and of artists and was greatly admired for its beauty. Munich was also a centre of Christian Romanticism and a place where the sciences flourished. The house of the ducal family, "Palais Max", stood in Ludwigstrasse, a *via triumphalis* of aristocratic and monumental buildings in the expanding city. Elisabeth was born into this world, here she grew up, in Munich her interest in art was stimulated and the foundations of her education were laid. Artistic and intellectual activities would help her to withstand the difficult period of her inner exile as empress of Austria.

Elisabeth had an older brother, Ludwig, and two younger brothers, the much-beloved Karl Theodor and Maximilian Emanuel, 12 years younger than her, as well as four sisters. Helena, nicknamed Nené - three years older than Elisabeth and from 1858 wife of the crown prince of Thurn and Taxis - was probably the closest to her. Two younger sisters married princes of the royal house of Bourbon and went to live under the southern sun. In 1859 Maria became queen of the Two Sicilies and in 1861 Mathilde became the duchess of Trani. Both soon suffered the fate of their deposed sovereigns. In 1860 Garibaldi landed in Sicily with his Army of a Thousand, entered Palermo and separated the island from the kingdom. Shortly afterwards Garibaldi expelled king Francesco II from Naples too and in February 1861, at Gaeta, forced him to capitulate. The unity of Italy was almost won. The brave young queen Maria, to whose aid her sister vainly attempted to run, went down in history as the heroine of Gaeta.

Her mother's brothers, because of their elevated social and political position, played an important role in the life of the children. The half-brother, king Ludwig I, was a fascinating and remarkably talented man. Because of his relationship with the ballerina Lola Montez he abdicated in the year of the revolution, 1848, and lived for another 20 years as a private citizen; this caused a great deal of controversy and aroused the sympathetic solidarity of Elisabeth.

In 1832 the youngest of king Ludwig's children, Otto, had been appointed ruler of the new, free kingdom of Greece, a significant episode that evoked romantic thoughts and sentiments in Elisabeth.

Elisabeth, however, was not in close personal relations with him, nor was she with the crown prince Maximilian or with prince Luitpold, both many years older than her.

Nor even did the next generation of Wittelsbach cousins play a significant role in the lives of Sissy and her brothers and sisters, not so much because they spent long periods far from the court of Munich, but because the "royals" were much younger. The fabulous king Ludwig II of Bavaria - who became sadly famous for the excesses of his building activity, for his insanely romantic obsession for opulence and his Wagnerian extravagances - was about eight years younger than Elisabeth, appearing on her horizon when she had already been empress of Austria for some time. They were, however, closer spiritually than Elisabeth ever wanted to acknowledge. Whether you like Heinrich Heine or Richard Wagner, the contrast is only apparent.

In 1824 her mother's elder sister, princess Sophia, had

married the archduke Franz Karl, brother of the future emperor Ferdinand of Austria. One day, in Vienna, this aunt of Elisabeth's would become her mother-in-law - a mother-in-law she would feel little love for, as is well known.
Of course, no one thought at all about this dynastic constellation as Elisabeth spent her happy and carefree childhood and youth in Munich and in Possenhofen. Elisabeth's mother Ludovica, to whom she always remained very attached, loved a simple, family life, without any great retinue of followers or social duties.

Elisabeth's father, Max, was a man who loved life, who was always ready to assume popular attitudes and dressed in the costume of Upper Bavaria. He was often travelling, and therefore entrusted the education of his eight children to their mother. When their father was present, however, he entertained the older ones as well as the younger ones, singing, playing the cithara, reciting poetry and playing with the children in the park.
Max was a passionate horserider and in the palace at Munich had a riding-ground installed. When he performed

Munich, Ludwigstrasse with the church of St Ludwig built by Friedrich Gärtner (1829-1844), the palace of duke Maximilian and, in the background, the Feldherrnhalle. Siderography by C. Geyer, ca. 1850.

Duke Max wearing the costume of Upper Bavaria while playing the cithara. By Leo Schöninger, ca. 1850.

The duchess Ludovica with her children Ludwig, Helena and the newborn Elisabeth. Lithograph by Ernst Kaiser, 1838.

there in the company of circus folk, it must certainly have been entertaining for his children, but aristocratic society judged his conduct with disapproval. Elisabeth, nicknamed Sissy, was a sensitive girl with a lively imagination; like her father she loved country life and preferred to stay at Lake Starnberg, since at Possenhofen, the family's idyllic summer residence, she was always allowed to keep a dozen animals. She also emulated her father's equestrian ambitions. Courtly education in the traditional sense of the term was perhaps rather neglected. Elisabeth's predilection for popular or sentimental poetry, as well as for Heinrich Heine, can probably be attributed to the romantic environment and the impressions of her childhood. What she later claimed to be a love of freedom was not only for the most part bookish, the result of romantic reading; it was also an arrogance projected into a childhood free of restrictions. Because obviously Elisabeth was and remained the knowing daughter of a sovereign family of German princes, she knew what life was at the royal court in Munich and was educated for an exclusive court life, but evidently it was not enough to ensure that she would be able to tolerate the pedantry and restraint of the imperial court in Vienna.

In the end, however, Elisabeth never really wanted to escape from her social environment: she remained a princess, an empress, a queen, all she wanted was to be free in her sentiments. Years later she would be accompanied on her innumerable long journeys by dozens of servants, and would almost always expect every sort of comfort.

The archduke Franz Joseph at the age of sixteen, colonel of a regiment of dragoons. Watercolour by Moritz Michael Daffinger from the guest book of the princess Melanie Metternich, 1846.

BAVARIA AND AUSTRIA AT THE DAWN OF THE 1848 REVOLUTION

At Possenhofen, as in Munich, reigned an atmosphere that was typical of German romanticism, where nature and landscape, traditions and patriotic sentiment had a significant influence in addition to their purely political importance. After the Napoleonic Wars, the German provinces had become autonomous states freely associated in the "German Confederation"; now they had their problems of differentiation.
Philistine patriotism was therefore encouraged. An example of this were the preparations for the wedding of the crown prince Maximilian in 1842, which were clearly designed to be a stylized reproduction of peasant clothing and the definition of "national" characteristics which in substance did not exist. In the Austrian empire, on the other hand, there could be no impulse to cultivate regional or national characteristics, since in the numerous kingdoms and countries which the emperor in Vienna ruled over, a dozen languages were spoken, as many religions and faiths were believed in and an infinite number of customs and traditions were cultivated. Therefore only faith in the "reigning house by hereditary right" could be the common link uniting the people. Austrian patriotism was necessarily of a dynastic character. When a younger generation, in the spirit of German romanticism, demanded the cultural autonomy of the people, patriotism was suddenly transformed into that fatal nationalism which undermined the existence of the Habsburg plurinational state and from then on gave Europe one war after another. The stratified and to our contemporary eyes indissoluble problems of the Austrian empire therefore loomed from the very beginning like a cloud over the formation of the young archduke Franz Joseph Karl, the cousin of Elisabeth and her future husband. He had been baptized with the names of three emperors. His ambitious mother Sophia, the princess Wittelsbach, must have had a great dynastic career in mind for him from the time of his birth (18 August 1830), and his new father, the archduke Franz Karl, was only too happy that finally, after almost six years of marriage and two miscarriages, his wife had given birth to a healthy boy. The archduke Franz Karl was the youngest child of the reigning emperor Franz I of Austria, and therefore brother of the successor to the throne Ferdinand. The latter, however, was certainly incapable of reigning, nor was it possible to expect any descendants from him, so

Princess Elisabeth, portrayed at the age of seven at Possenhofen. Wooden bust, originally probably painted, by Anton Fernkorn, 1845, conserved at the Hofburg in Vienna.

for the newborn Franzi, as he was soon nicknamed, loomed the prospect of an inevitable future of responsibility. However, "Kaiser Franz" became the godfather of his first "Habsburg" nephew.
The family of the archduke Franz Karl chose Schönbrunn as their favourite residence, and there the future emperor Franz Joseph spent most of his childhood and almost all his life. The family grew: in July 1832 Ferdinand Maximilian was born, the future emperor of Mexico, one year later Karl Ludwig, a sister then followed, Maria Anna, who died at the age of five, and lastly, in 1842, a fourth child, Ludwig Victor. The children grew up in a cordial environment, an almost bourgeois familiarity; their tutors were chosen with care, and they received an intense and strict education in the subjects then in vogue: religion, history, geography and languages; very soon a military training also began for Franzi. Colonel Hauslab trained him with the infantry regiment "Hoch- und Deutschmeister" in foot exercises, very soon he was appointed lieutenant and in 1843, therefore when only 13 years of age, colonel and leader of a regiment of dragoons. Throughout his life Franz Joseph's favourite dress was his military uniform.
Even before the paths of the young couple had crossed, Franz Joseph, not yet eighteen years old, had already lived through war and revolution and on 2 December 1848, under turbulent auspices, had acceded to the throne.
In March 1848, in Vienna as in other European capitals, a great socio-political revolution had broken out that threatened the cohesion of the Habsburg empire and monarchy. The emperor Ferdinand abdicated, the chancellor Metternich, who had always seemed omnipotent, resigned and was forced to flee. Hungary was overwhelmed with the help of Russian troops, and in other parts of the empire, for example in Vienna, recourse was made to the force of arms in order to re-establish the calm. In northern Italy war broke out against the kingdom of Sardinia, in the course of which Franz Joseph received his baptism of fire in the battle of Santa Lucia.
The reign of Franz Joseph began, therefore, in unfavourable circumstances. Those reponsible for the situation were essentially the men of the previous age, the so-called *Vormärz*, but in addition to this a shadow obscured the accession to the throne of the young sovereign who had been educated in the tradition of an anachronistic absolutism. Only years later would he find the counsellors who would lead him on the path towards liberal reforms, towards a form of constitutional government and consequently towards national freedom.

The castle of Possenhofen on Lake Starnberg. Gouache from an album of Elisabeth, dated 3 April 1854.

Franz Joseph dressed as a hunter, with a short-barrelled shot-gun held with both hands, against the background of an Alpine landscape. Lithograph from an original photograph.

Elisabeth, portrait of the bride against the beautiful background landscape of Lake Starnberg. Lithograph on clay by Eduard Kaiser, 1853/54.

A period print which became popular shows an idyllic scene: the newly-wed couple - Elisabeth dressed in Tyrolese costume and Franz Joseph wearing a jacket, knee-length leather breeches and a hat adorned with Alpine flowers and pheasant feathers - together with Duke Max, dressed in the same way, on a raft on Lake Starnberg; Franz Joseph is rowing while Max plays the cithara. Lithograph by Anton Schlögl, 1854.

ENGAGEMENT AND MARRIAGE - SISSY BECOMES EMPRESS

In 1848, the two sisters Helena and Elisabeth met their Austrian cousins at Innsbruck, and soon afterwards it was arranged that Helena would marry the young emperor Franz Joseph. The engagement was supposed to have taken place in 1853 at Ischl. The place of the first meeting was a rented villa which was later bought and transformed into "Kaiservilla" for the family's annual holidays. But during this time, as many accounts have related, Franz Joseph fell madly in love with the not yet sixteen year-old Sissy, and all the carefully laid plans of her mother and aunt were foiled. On 18 August, the day of his twenty-third birthday, Franz Joseph became engaged with Elisabeth, and not with Helena.

The two young fiancés had a year before the wedding. For Franz Joseph this year was filled with politics, for Elisabeth with various preparations that were necessary in view of her imminent and unexpected elevated social position. She had to make up for the many shortcomings in her education, she had to learn not only international languages but also at least one of the most important Austrian languages, that is, Czech, and she also had to prepare a large ceremonial trousseau. When two dynasties of princes come together in marriage various questions of public and ecclesiastical law need to be settled. Because of the close kinship of the two spouses a papal dispensation was required for the marriage, and Elisabeth had to renounce any possible claims deriving from her albeit distant membership of the royal house of Bavaria.

Franz Joseph visited his fiancée several times in Possenhofen and Munich, and finally, on 20 April 1854, Elisabeth set off for the wedding. From Munich she went to Regensburg and from there, on the Danube, to Vienna by way of Linz; she stayed the night in Schönbrunn and on 24 April she made her entrance into the church of St Augustine for the marriage ceremony. This was followed

The newly-wed couple against the background of a park. Franz Joseph wearing his fieldmarshal's uniform, Elisabeth an ermine cloak. Miniature on porcelain, Viennese workmanship, 1854, conserved at the Hofburg in Vienna.

Excursion of the couple on the day of their engagement (18 August 1853) in the environs of Bad Ischl. The emperor's field adjutant, count Grünne, leads six dappled horses in the hunting outing. Painting (ca. 1855) conserved at the Wagenburg in Schönbrunn.

Elisabeth's so-called wedding eve dress, probably worn for a farewell evening in Munich. Organza, green silk, stole embroidered with Turkish decorative motifs, the property of her lady-in-waiting in Munich. Now at the Monturdepot in Vienna.

Elisabeth's departure from the family house in Munich on 20 April 1854. The bride, in an open carriage, passes under the triumphal arch, just completed in 1852, on her way to Regensburg. Lithograph by Alexander Ziegler from Johann Schmuckl, Vienna, 1854.

Elisabeth's arrival at Nusdorf near Vienna on 22 April 1854. The bride arrives from Linz on board the steamship "Franz Joseph" and is welcomed by her husband. Lithograph by Vinzenz Katzler, 1854.

Elisabeth's official entrance into Vienna on 23 April 1854. The bride and her mother, the duchess Ludovica, in Napoleon's "Lombard coronation carriage", today conserved at the Wagenburg in Schönbrunn, pass the River Wien at the Karlsplatz on the newly-built "Elisabethbrücke". Lithograph by F. Kollarz, 1854.

View of Vienna, in the foreground the area in front of the Hofburg with the fortifications on both sides of the gate and the bastion, dating from before 1860. Watercolour by Franz Alt, 1873.

by an incredible number of festivities, receptions and audiences. Hardly even aware of it, Elisabeth suddenly found herself immersed in the pedantic formalities of life at the Viennese court. Her aunt and mother-in-law Sophia now became her unbearable teacher in life. In the space of just a few days Elisabeth came to realize that she had completely lost her youthly independence, and that at the Viennese court her poetic sense of freedom was destined to languish. Elisabeth was the empress, but at the Hofburg Sophia reigned supreme. Spurred by the ambition of turning her sixteen year-old niece Sissy into a perfect empress and by preoccupations about her beloved son, Sophia despotically and tactlessly interfered in all the young couple's affairs. This disagreeable state of affairs began immediately after the first wedding night, at the breakfast table, which Elisabeth fled from in tears. A few days later the couple escaped to Laxenburg, where they spent a brief honeymoon. Then Franz Joseph resumed his daily visits to the city while his wife remained alone at Laxenburg. Elisabeth avoided the Hofburg and the people who laid down the law there, and in a poem desribed it as a prison. From the very beginning Elisabeth felt nostalgia for Possenhofen and a yearning for the big wide world.

She never got used to her role as the ruler of an empire of forty million inhabitants, a role involving numerous ceremonial, charitable and family obligations. She always chose situations which corresponded to her state of mind at the time, alternating between a totally secluded life and

The empress's wedding-dress. Illustration taken from the fashion magazine «L'Iris», 1854. This charming image can certainly not claim to faithfully reproduce the wedding-dress, nor can the portrait be said to resemble the empress.

The train of Elisabeth's wedding-dress, silk rep with refined gold embroidery. Property of her daughter Maria Valeria, now at the Kunsthistorisches Museum in Vienna.

The Michaelerplatz with the winter riding school and the old Burgtheater. Watercolour by Rudolf von Alt, 1880. At the time of Elisabeth's wedding, the side of the Hofburg facing the city was not at all grandiose in appearance. The bride was accustomed instead to the sumptuous new buildings of the artistic city of Munich. The facade overlooking the Michaelerplatz was completed in its present form only in 1893. (cf. ill. on p. 33).

Marriage of Franz Joseph and Elisabeth in the church of St Augustine on 24 April 1854. The archbishop of Vienna, Cardinal Rauscher, presents the wedding rings to the couple. Lithograph by Vinzenz Katzler entitled "Austria's greatest day", 1854.

periods of intense political commitment, between an arrogant contempt for humanity and a sympathetic interest in the ill and wounded. The conflict between the affection she felt for her husband and family relationships on the one hand and her desire for independence and nostalgia for remote lands on the other tormented her and quickly condemned her to a life of solitude, a solitude accentuated by the fact that the emperor was absorbed throughout his life by often petty political matters and by the bureaucratic affairs of his ministers. In the Hofburg he was exposed to the influence of his counsellors and the court society, who were only too ready to enviously criticize and denigrate the young empress.

Elisabeth during the first year of her marriage. Painting by Franz Schrotzberg, ca. 1855.

Frontispiece with dedication to Elisabeth. For the wedding of the imperial couple, the Viennese music publisher Carl Anton Spina had a collection of images of regional costumes and songs of the Austrian crown territories compiled, which he dedicated to the young empress. Austrian National Library.

Ihrer Majestät
der
Kaiserin Elisabeth
von Oesterreich etc.
in tiefster Ehrfurcht
dargebracht
von C. A. Spina
k. k. Hof u. pr. Kunst u. Musikalienhændler
Brünn.
Pesth.
Innsbruck.
Prag.
Lemberg.
Triest.
Mailand.
WIEN.
Venedig.

Open imperial "Victoria" type ceremonial carriage, with a team of four dappled horses bridled "à la Daumont", jockeys and footman on horseback, in the park of Laxenburg. Oil painting, ca. 1860, at the Wagenburg in Schönbrunn.

The imperial couple during a horse ride in the park of Lainz near Vienna. Franz Joseph wears the uniform of colonel belonging to his regiment of uhlans. Coloured lithograph by Eduard Kaiser, 1854/55.

Elisabeth riding a carriage, accompanied by one of her dogs, in the park of Laxenburg. Watercolour in the style of Alexander von Bensa, ca. 1865.

The newly-wed imperial couple. Franz Joseph is wearing his fieldmarshal's gala uniform, Elisabeth an ermine fur. Coloured lithograph by Eduard Kaiser, 1856.

Three generations of the imperial family. The archduchess Sophia holds her newborn grand-daughter Gisela, whose parents, Elisabeth and Franz Joseph, are portrayed with their daughter Sophia; the archduke Franz Karl is standing behind them. Lithograph on clay by Josef Bauer, 1856.

Journey of the imperial couple in the kingdom of Lombardy-Veneto, to reconcile the anti-Austrian forces and win over the Italians to the cause of a common Austria. After a celebratory function, Franz Joseph and Elisabeth leave the cathedral of San Marco in Venice.

ELISABETH AND HER CHILDREN

Elisabeth received firm support from her husband and Franz Joseph even attempted to impose his will on his mother, but his governmental affairs, in the context of a highly difficult political situation, absorbed him almost entirely. From the year of the revolution, 1848, Europe had not had a moment of peace. Austria was particularly affected by changes in the Balkans. Following a vain attempt at mediation between Russia and Turkey in the controversy over the Danubian principalities, in 1853 Austria slipped into a foreign conflict in an unfavourable position.

Elisabeth with her children Gisela and Rudolph in Laxenburg castle. On the wall a portrait of her daughter Sophia, who died in 1857. Watercolour by Josef Kriehuber, 1858, at the Albertina in Vienna.

Elisabeth in a negligé, with her splendid long hair falling in tresses across her chest, 1864. This private portrait of the empress was executed by Franz Xaver Winterhalter at the same time as official and semi-official state portraits (cf. pp. 29 and 30). This image of Elisabeth bathed in morning light remained hanging above the desk of the emperor Franz Joseph for the rest of his life (cf. p. 52).

When Franz Joseph, on the side of Turkey, England and France, entered the so-called Crimean War against Russia in 1854 he irreconcilably made himself an enemy of the tsar. The Balkans was where the spheres of influence of two empires, Russia and Austria, bordered each other. Almost the whole peninsula was still under Turkish rule. Only Greece had become independent in 1830, and was governed (until 1862) by king Otto I of the house of Wittelsbach, a cousin of both Franz Joseph and Elisabeth. The Serbs, with the support of Russia and Austria had, from the 18th century, already obtained a certain autonomy within the Ottoman kingdom, despite the fact that the two great powers had sustained different Serbian leaders. From the 1850s there was growing demand not only to free the Serbs and Croats from Turkish rule, but also to reunite them in a single state together with those who lived in Austria-Hungary.
In March 1855 the first-born child of the imperial couple was born,

Sophia, who died in Budapest in 1857 at the age of only two. In the meantime, in July 1856, the empress had given birth to a second daughter, Gisela. However, few people seemed to be in any doubt about the personal happiness of the imperial couple. If the political horizon appeared gloomy, Elisabeth's future prospects as a wife and mother seemed equally bleak. In August 1858 she gave birth to the much longed-for male child and heir to the throne. He was baptized with the name of Rudolph, just like the dynasty's royal ancestor.

Elisabeth in the autumn of 1860. Shortly after this, in November, mentally distressed and unhappy, she fled from the court of Vienna. Photograph by Ludwig Angerer.

Elisabeth wearing her ballroom dress, with the great set of emeralds which were part of the family jewels of the Habsburg-Lorraine dynasties. Painting by Franz Russ, 1863, at the castle of Schönbrunn.

Madeira, autumn 1860. Elisabeth, playing the mandolin, surrounded by the ladies-in-waiting countess Hunyady (left), princess Windisch-Graetz (right) and princess Thurn and Taxis (in the foreground). All four are dressed almost identically, an imaginative variation of a sailor's costume.

Red velvet robe-manteau, lavishly decorated with gold embroidery and gilded passamanerie. Gift for Elisabeth on the occasion of one of her journeys in the Near East. Private property.

By this time the empress had exhausted her mental and physical energies. She could no longer tolerate life at court or politics and she had estranged herself from the family to such an extent that in the summer of 1860 she abandoned Vienna and travelled for two years, despite the fact that at the time Rudolph was only two years old and Gisela only four. As for Elisabeth, she was not even twenty-two! First she took refuge in Bavaria and stayed with her family whom she had not visited for years.
In the autumn she left Vienna again and, accompanied by Franz Joseph as far as Bamberg, journeyed to Antwerp. She travelled clandestinely, though with her retinue of 27 people she used a steamship of the British royal navy for the tempestuous crossing to Madeira. Among those accompanying her were the ladies-in-waiting portrayed here and their husbands, the empress's "knights of honour"; also among them were count Hohenstein, count Szápáry and prince Rudolph Liechtenstein, a man she particularly esteemed. Later she would call him, in Hungarian, "Szépherczeg", that is, "handsome prince". In Madeira count Hunyady fell in love with the empress and was immediately sent back to Vienna. From various sources we learn that few men were able to resist the empress's charm, when she was not completely absorbed in herself. Not only was Elisabeth conscious of the attraction she exerted; she also learnt how to use this power. In Madeira, far from the Viennese court, free from official obligations and the private tyranny of her mother-in-law, surrounded by a luxuriant natural environment and by people who liked her, and generously supplied by Franz Joseph with unlimited financial means, Elisabeth recovered her mental and physical

strength and found herself again. In the April of the following year, after eight months away, she left the island and, passing through Cadiz, Seville, Gibraltar, Majorca and Malta, visited Corfu, then an English possession. Only in October did she see Franz Joseph and her children again in Venice.

Perhaps her love for Franz Joseph had faded; the fact is that inside herself she felt that she was the stronger of the two. How little solidarity she demonstrated to her husband, how little sense of responsibility she showed towards the public, a public forced to witness with dismay the country's political and military defeats.

When Elisabeth finally returned to the Viennese court in the summer of 1862 she was a different person. Now she manifested a certain participation in public events, since they seemed to promise new political opportunities for the dynasty and the kingdom.

On the other hand Elisabeth had to feel also personally involved in political developments, and henceforth it was like this for everything concerning Hungary. She was particularly upset by the intentions of her beloved brother-in-law Maximilian to launch himself into a Mexican venture which Elisabeth judged to be utterly senseless. In April 1864 the archduke, with his wife Charlotte, a Belgian princess of the house of Saxe-Coburg-Gotha, departed from Miramare on the frigate "Novara", headed for Mexico, where Maximilian accepted the imperial crown. In this way he put himself at the service of the politics of Napoleon III of France. In the same period Franz Joseph convened a meeting of German princes in Frankfurt to revive the Germanic Confederation. However, the new organization of German kingdoms and provinces to which he aspired came to nothing because the powerful prime minister Bismarck dissuaded his king, William I of Prussia, from participating in the meeting. The Prussian chancellor wanted instead to expel Austria from the Germanic Confederation and

Madeira, spring 1861. Elisabeth as she goes to church in Funchal. Lithograph by Adolph Dauthage from a photograph by Angerer of 1860 (cf. ill. p. 24).

Queen Maria Sophia of the Two Sicilies, Elisabeth's younger sister, around 1860. Due to her fearless conduct during the defence of the last stronghold against Garibaldi's troops, she was called the heroine of Gaeta.

Elisabeth in a happier period of her life, absorbed by her interest in Hungary, its history and its language. During this period she embodied the contemporary ideal of beauty. Photograph by Ludwig Angerer, ca. 1865.

Elisabeth wearing a ballroom dress made by the French tailor Worth, and with diamond-encrusted stars in her hair made by the court jeweller of Vienna Alexander Emmanuel Köchert. In 1864 the emperor Franz Joseph commissioned three portraits of the empress to the internationally renowned German painter Xaver Winterhalter, who had also portrayed Elisabeth's rival in beauty, the empress Eugenie, wife of the French emperor Napoleon III.

Elisabeth in profile, with her hair let down as far as her hips. Painting by Franz Xaver Winterhalter, 1864. This portrait which was, so to speak, semi-official, was hung in the emperor's study at the Hofburg, where it has remained to this day.

Elisabeth, proud and beautiful, in the happy years following the birth of her youngest and best-loved child, Maria Valeria. Photograph by Ludwig Angerer, ca. 1870.

Franz Joseph in his Austrian fieldmarshal's gala uniform, with the Order of the Golden Fleece, the stars of the four orders of the Austrian ruling family, the sash of the military order of Maria Theresa and the cross of the Russian order of St George (4th class), in 1864. This painting by Franz Xaver Winterhalter, a full-length official state portrait, is the companion-piece of the empress in evening dress (ill. p. 29).

The wing of the Hofburg overlooking the Michaelerplatz was built, on designs made around 1730 by Joseph Emanuel Fischer von Erlach for the emperor Charles VI, only under the emperor Franz Joseph, and completed around 1895. This facade, therefore, never became familiar to Elisabeth.

Schönbrunn, built around 1700 on a design by Johann Bernhard Fischer von Erlach for the emperor Joseph I and modified under Maria Theresa by Nikolaus Pacassi, was the imperial family's summer residence. Franz Joseph was born here in 1830, and here in 1916 he died. View of the central wing of the facade overlooking the garden, with the northern outskirts of Vienna in the background.

At the Hofburg, the empress Elisabeth lived in the so-called apartments of Alexander in the Amalienhof. They had been furnished in the middle of the 18th century, but the furnishings were continually renewed, and this was also done in 1856/57 for the newly-wed imperial couple. In the saloon and bedroom of the empress we see in the background the iron bed which was taken into the room in the evening.

The former toilette, due to the presence of sports training equipment, is today also called the "gymnastics room". Here we can also see paintings of her beloved circus horses and some of her dogs.

Both photographs date from 1943.

Elisabeth's circus horses, Flic and Floc. Painting by the horse painter Wilhelm Richter, much esteemed at the Viennese court, 1877. In the building of the court stables the empress had a riding-ground, which had been built on the orders of Franz Joseph next to the great winter riding school. A small riding-ground had also been included in the Villa of Hermes next to the stables, where Elisabeth perfected her equestrian skills. In 1875 she had taken dressage lessons from Elise Petzold, daughter of the circus-owner Ernst J. Remy, and two years later she was instructed in the art of "high school" at the Spanish riding school.

"Portraits" of some of Elisabeth's favourite dogs, executed in around 1873 by the animal painter Carl Reichert; above, Hamlet, Fanton and Morphy, below, Roma and Brave.

Horseriding hunts with large packs of dogs, according to the English model, were a favourite recreation of the high aristocracy also in Austria-Hungary. A painting by Julius von Blaas of 1878 shows Elisabeth and Franz Joseph during a horse hunt in the Göding estate in Moravia.

Elisabeth riding side-saddle with close-fitting riding-habit jumps over a hedge during a chase. Siderography by F. L. Alkinson from an unknown painting, ca. 1880.

unify Germany under the leadership of Prussia. In 1866 he found a pretext for realizing this ambition with force. In the battle of Königgrätz Austria was routed by the Prussian army and the Germanic Confederation was dissolved.
In the autumn of 1864, the greatly acclaimed and highly sought-after German painter Franz Xaver Winterthaler came to Vienna from Paris and painted two full-length state portraits of the emperor and empress, as well as two intimate half-figure portraits of the empress, which Franz Joseph had hanging in his study until the end of his life. The emperor found master Winterthaler very sure of himself and the price of his paintings rather high.

Elisabeth adored English dogs and gave English names to her German boar-hounds. Around 1873 the painter Carl Reichert was commissioned to execute portraits of numerous dogs, which were "humbly presented" in a folder "to Her Majesty the empress and queen Elisabeth". Evidently Reichert painted them in part from life, as can be seen from the fine photograph of the empress with her terrier Oscar, executed around 1868 by Emil Rabending; on the right the boar-hound Dragon. When Elisabeth's favourite dog, Shadow, a black German boar-hound, died, he was buried in the park of Gödöllö castle.

Coronation procession, 8 June 1867. Franz Joseph on horseback in traditional Hungarian national costume, Elisabeth in the "imperial carriage", the Baroque carriage of the coronation of the Habsburg house, in front of the portal of the church of St Matthew at Ofen.

Elisabeth in her coronation dress in silver brocade and black velvet bodice, in the style of a Hungarian national costume (cf. also ill p. 40). Photograph by Emil Rabending, 1867.

Coronation of Franz Joseph and Elisabeth with the crown of St Stephen of Hungary. Count Gyula Andrássy pronounces the first "Éljen" (hurrah). Siderography by Eugen Doby from a painting by Eduard Engerth in the castle of Budapest.

ELISABETH - QUEEN OF HUNGARY

In the spring of 1867 negotiations between the imperial government and representatives of the Hungarian magnates ended and the much-debated "compromise" between the two "halves" of the Habsburg empire was established. The Austrian empire, which had existed since 1804 as a single state governed by an absolute sovereign, became the dual monarchy of Austria-Hungary. The divided empire had a supreme head, the emperor and king, and ministers that were both in common and separate, presided over by prime ministers in Vienna and in Budapest. The two halves of the empire shared a single minister for foreign affairs, a minister of war and a minister of finances.

The glorious manifestation of this long-contested but also conquered unity was the coronation of Franz Joseph and Elisabeth as apostolic king and queen of Hungary.

Celebrations took place at the beginning of June 1867. The ancient, traditional Hungarian city of coronations, Pressburg (in Hungarian Pozsony) was not chosen, but instead the ambitious metropolis of Budapest which had been born from the union of the two cities Ofen (Buda) and Pest, respectively on the right and left bank of the Danube. Like Vienna, Pest particularly had completely modified its appearance thanks to a generous policy of public and private building activity. The celebrated parliament, today the dominant building on the Danube, could not be built, however, until Hungary had been granted its own government.

The coronation of the king and queen in the church of St Matthew in the castle was a medieval feast, whose participants dressed in magnificent clothes, costumes and uniforms, with gem-encrusted arms, feathered hats and fur-fringed dolmans, high on their horses. It was perhaps the last great feast of old Europe, and became a triumph for Elisabeth. It would be true to say that a vital role in the achievement of the "compromise" with Hungary was attributable to her. Elisabeth loved the country and the people, she had learnt the Hungarian language to perfection

The queen of Hungary. Elisabeth wearing her coronation dress. Painting by Georg Raab at the Hofburg in Vienna, 1867.

Millennium of the kingdom of Hungary. At the emperor's side, Elisabeth, wearing a black silk dress, appears for the last time in Hungary at the inauguration of the "millennium celebrations", 8 June 1896. Detail from a painting by Julius Benczúr.

The royal family in the park of Gödöllö. Franz Joseph wearing the Austrian version of the fieldmarshall's campaign uniform, Elisabeth and her children Rudolph, Gisela and Maria Valeria.
Coloured lithograph by Vinzenz Katzler, 1871.

Elisabeth with her son Rudolph during a sleigh ride in Hungary. From a drawing by Theodor Breitwiser, 1876.

Elisabeth in folkloristic dress, 1863. Coloured lithograph by Emile Desmaisons from a painting by Franz Russ.

and maintained close contacts with Hungarian statesmen, poets and scholars. The most prominent of these figures was count Gyula Andrássy, a gallant man who came to exert a decisive influence on Elisabeth. Andrássy had behind him a life that in those days would have been possible only in Austria. Due to his active participation in the Hungarian revolution against the Habsburg imperial house of 1848 he had been condemned to death, but had escaped to western Europe and reentered Hungary only after having been pardoned. He was also called the "Beau Pendu", the handsome hanged man! After the compromise he became the first Hungarian president of ministers and later even foreign minister of the Austro-Hungarian empire. The Hungarians adored their Elisa-

The archduchess Gisela at the age of sixteen with her husband, duke Leopold of Bavaria, in the circle of the imperial family. The little Maria Valeria, as in many other instances, is embracing a large dog. Lithograph from a photomontage, 1872.

Court ball in the hall of ceremonies of the Viennese Hofburg, 28 January 1886. On the left, the empress attends the reception with her niece Stephanie, on the right the crown prince alone and in the centre the emperor. From an original by Wilhelm Gause.

beth, even until well after her death. After the coronation, the king Franz Joseph and queen Elisabeth received as a gift the hunting castle of Gödöllö, east of Budapest. Elisabeth had previously shown interest in it and had wanted to purchase it. For its part, the royal couple assigned the nation's gift for the coronation - 100,000 florins - to the widows and orphans of the soldiers who had fought against Austria in 1848/49. Every year the "royal" family spent several weeks at Gödöllö. The castle stood in a beautiful large hunting reserve, an ideal place for horseriding, which Elisabeth used intensely on her own, but also frequently with numerous guests, her English and Hungarian friends, as well as with the more experienced riders of the family, therefore with her husband Franz

Easter 1870. Elisabeth (left) and Franz Joseph (right) at the feet-washing ceremony on Easter Thursday, in the hall of ceremonies of the Viennese Hofburg. From a drawing by Vinzenz Katzler.

Elisabeth, together with the German empress Augusta, wife of William I, is paid homage at the feast of count Andrássy in 1873. On her right, standing in the background, the fieldmarshall archduke Albert, the emperor Franz Joseph, and the host, at that time foreign minister.

Elisabeth in ballroom dress wearing the jewels of rubies redesigned for her, in 1854, from a set consisting of diadem, neckband, necklace, breast-piece and ear-rings, coming from the legacy of queen Marie Antoinette and belonging to the personal jewels of the imperial family. Painting by Georg Raab, ca. 1878/79, conserved at the Bundesmobiliendepot.

Joseph and later with the crown prince Rudolph.
In April 1868, as evidence of a refound conjugal happiness, Elisabeth gave birth in Budapest to a daughter, Maria Valeria. She was very attached to the child, and from this time on did nothing without her. During these years a charming series of photos were taken of the empress and queen, both in Budapest on the occasion of the coronation and later in Vienna. Masterfully composed portraits show the woman who had barely turned thirty in the fullness of her beauty, a beauty counter-balanced by a seriousness full of sentiment.
A comparison with the portraits of her son Rudolph reveals the profound affinity that existed between them.
The great family feasts came in the 1870s. Elisabeth returned to taking part in public ceremonies, especially in Hungary, and appeared at court balls. Summers were spent partly at Ischl with her family, and partly at Gödöllö, where she devoted much of her time to riding.
In 1874 she went for the first time (together with Maria Valeria) to England, where in later years she dedicated herself almost exclusively to exhausting and sometimes dangerous hunts on horseback.
In spring 1872 the archduchess Gisela, little more than a girl, had become engaged to her Wittelsbach cousin Leopold, ten years older, the son of the future prince regent of Bavaria Luitpold. Elisabeth was not happy with the union but had little influence over her eldest daughter, who had been estranged from her at an early age by the archduchess Sophia. It had been Elisabeth herself who had entrusted the upbringing of her daughter to others in the decisive years of her escape from the Viennese court.

THE VILLA OF HERMES

In 1882, the celebrated architect Carl von Hasenauer - who in those years had been busy on the building of the two imperial museums on the Ringstrasse and on the enlargement of the Hofburg - received from the emperor the commission to build for Elisabeth, in the imperial hunting reserve of Lainz near Vienna, a formal villa which responded more to her personal taste than to that of the poetic empress.

However the pictorial decoration reflected her tastes at least as much as the subjects. Elisabeth's favourite play was Shakespeare's *A Midsummer Night's Dream*, and in her poems and letters she had several times identified herself with the fairy-queen Titania. In every castle she lived in she wanted an image of Titania with the ass, something she justified with self-critical spirit, declaring that she "never tired of looking at the ass's head of our sentiments, which we fondle without respite".

Elisabeth also purchased paintings in later years, for example for the Villa of Hermes Venetian motifs, following more the romantic predilections of her Wittelsbach cousin king Ludwig II of Bavaria than the official taste of Franz Joseph.

The neo-Baroque building was at first supposed to be named "Villa Waldruh", but later, from a marble statue of Hermes by Ernst Herter, it was called the Villa of Hermes. From 1866 the empress regularly spent many weeks of the year there, until 1891 when the Achilleion of Corfu, executed according to her wishes and to her ideas, became for a short time her favourite residence.

Elisabeth's bedchamber in the Villa of Hermes. On the ceiling of the sumptuously furnished and decorated room, a painting by Hans Makart represents the kingdom of the fairy queen Titania, hovering in the air before Oberon's tigers.

The gymnastics room with lavish wall paintings in the Pompeiian style. On the walls various sports are represented, above the doors a racing contest and a stag hunt painted by August Eisenmenger, while the still lifes on the skirting-board are by Hugo Charlemont.

Villa Waldruh.

The empress, with a sudden gesture, hides her face behind a fan to avoid the intrusive attentions of a photographer.

THE HORSERIDER

Franz Joseph and Elisabeth did not have a great deal in common other than their early love. Both however were excellent riders and loved horses and carriages. However, what for a young aristocrat of military training was taken for granted, Elisabeth had to cultivate in the face of all social prejudices. Not only did she ride at her husband's side in the hunting chases; she was the only woman to sustain extremely difficult obstacle courses in England and Ireland. In 1874, during her first visit to England, she became acquainted with the international society of horse hunts and races, and received as a gift an English hunting horse. The following year, in England, Elisabeth suffered concussion following a bad fall from a horse, and from 1876 Bay Middleton became her irreplaceable guide. In the 1870s she tirelessly practised racing and horse-jumping, both in the Viennese Freudenau and at Gödöllö, and kept a large stable of mostly Irish and English horses. In 1875 she took lessons in dressage from the daughter of the proprietor of the Renz circus, and in 1877 was introduced to the long-established rudiments of the classical "high school" at the Spanish riding school. Quite apart from her exceptional equestrian talent, however, Elisabeth on horseback was a devastatingly beautiful and elegant sight.

Elisabeth with "English style" riding-habit (with top-hat). A painting by the famous horse-painter Wilhelm Richter, 1876.

Franz Joseph and Elisabeth at breakfast in the empress's saloon.

Franz Joseph at his desk in the studio at the Hofburg. In front of him the most intimate of the portraits of the empress executed in 1864 by Franz Xaver Winterhalter (cf. ill. p. 22).

Two drawings by Theo Zaschke, ca. 1890, for the celebratory volume Viribus Unitis.

Elisabeth's apartments at the Hofburg, which in the years of her youth she never liked but which later she had furnished according to her own tastes, particularly with numerous portraits of her children, her brothers and her sisters. The photographs were probably taken shortly after the empress's death.

On 31 January 1876 Elisabeth places a wreath on the tomb of Ferenc Deák. The empress greatly admired the Hungarian liberal politician and judge of the constitutional court, who was called the "wise man of the Hungarian nation". From a drawing by Vinzenz Katzler.

Black gala dress in moiré silk and black lace belonging to the empress Elisabeth, worn around 1878.

THE EMPRESS'S CLOTHES

In the house of Habsburg it was not the custom to keep either the precious clothes that had been worn for a marriage or a coronation, or the ceremonial clothes that had to be worn on all official occasions: they were instead given away to ladies-in-waiting or maidservants. Sometimes they were even made into ecclesiastical vestments. While men appeared year after year in their unchanging, splendid military or court uniforms, ladies were always dressed in the latest French fashions. Shoes and underclothing were worn on a single occasion, as were many clothes made of precious fabrics since they could not be washed. In this respect it is almost understandable that Elisabeth always took dozens of servants with her on her travels. And yet on one occasion she said: "They dress me with fine clothes and many jewels, I go out and exchange a few words with the people, then I hurry to my room, take off everything and write, and Heine guides my hand!".

Only a few of Elisabeth's clothes have been conserved, partly in Vienna, partly in Budapest, like the black gala dress reproduced here. The charming figure of the empress at the age of forty has been immortalized (also as regards fashion) in numerous portraits reproduced here by the painters Winterhalter, Russ or Raab, and in some photographs. It should not be forgotten however that painters and photographers knew how to flatter and retouch, and therefore to deceive.

Romantically transfigured portrait of the empress in Corfu, a posthumous painting by the Munich artist Friedrich August von Kaulbach. Pastel on paper after 1898, property of the empress's grand-daughter Elisabeth, the only daughter of the crown prince Rudolph.

THE ACHILLEION OF CORFU

Elisabeth had visited Corfu for the first time in 1861, not yet twenty-three years old. From this time on she was very fond of the island and visited it frequently, often stopping off on her travels in the eastern Mediterranean and Near East. She took intensive lessons in ancient and modern Greek with various teachers, some extremely erudite, one of whom, the young Constantine Christomanos, left pages of a diary that reveal much about Elisabeth's thoughts and feelings. But her most important mentor was the Austrian consul in Corfu, Alexander von Warsberg, one of the greatest experts on Greece and its history, who also assumed responsibility for the initial designs of the Achilleion. From 1888 Elisabeth had set her mind on building a palace on the island that was completed in 1891, and which even today is resplendent with seductive beauty. In the park the empress had a statue of the dying Achilles erected, as well as a small temple to her favourite poet, Heinrich Heine. However, almost as soon as the Achilleion was finished, Elisabeth lost all interest in it. She stayed there for the last time in April 1896.

·GRAND HOTEL BEAU-RIVAGE·

Assassination in Geneva. The Italian anarchist Luigi Lucheni, armed with a knife, lunges at the empress and her lady-in-waiting as they are about to take the steamboat back to Caux. Wood-engraving in a newspaper, September 1898.

In Vienna it was quickly decided to erect a monument to the empress. A poetical/sentimental design by Robert Weigl, showing Elisabeth hovering amid clouds, was never executed. The fine monument of the Volksgarten in Vienna was created by Hans Bitterlich and unveiled in 1907 in the presence of the emperor.

Bodice of the black taffeta and black lace dress that Elisabeth was wearing when she was assassinated. The property of her lady-in-waiting, countess Sztáray, the dress was later transferred to the "Queen Elisabeth Museum" in Budapest and, after the latter's destruction, to the Hungarian National Museum.

Elisabeth's funeral procession in front of the Hotel Beau-Rivage in Geneva.

DEATH AND APOTHEOSIS

During the last years of her life, journeys lasting many months took the morbidly restless empress through southern and central Europe and several times to Lake Geneva. In spring 1897 she came from the Riviera to Territet (Caux), where by chance she encountered the heir to the throne, archduke Franz Ferdinand, whose personal physician, doctor Eisenmenger, saw her and noted symptoms of oedema induced by hunger. In March 1898, and at the end of the summer, she again stayed at Territet. On 9 November, in the company of her trusted lady-in-waiting countess Sztáray and a small retinue, she went to visit baroness Julie Rothschild at Pregny, then spent the night in Geneva at the Grand Hotel Beau-Rivage, under the usual pseudonym of "countess of Hohenems". On 10 September Elisabeth was assassinated on the wharf. Franz Joseph was informed of the tragedy the same day.

On 11 September the autopsy and embalming were carried out and on 13 September the bishop of Freiburg imparted his blessing. On 15 September the body of the empress arrived at the Hofburg, and on 17 September was buried in the crypt of the Capuchins. Even the rosewood hotel bed where the empress had spent her last night was taken to Vienna.

CHRONOLOGY OF A RESTLESS LIFE

Short biography of the Empress Elisabeth

1837 Elisabeth Amelie Eugenie is born on 24 December in Munich, the fourth daughter of Duke Maximilian Joseph (Max) of Bavaria and his wife Louisa Wilhelmina (Ludovica).
1848 Visit to Innsbruck. Elisabeth meets two of her Austrian cousins, Franz Joseph and Karl Ludwig.
1853 18 August: engagement to the emperor Franz Joseph at Ischl.
1854 24 April: wedding in the church of St Augustine. Honeymoon in Laxenburg.
1855 Her daughter Sophia is born on 5 March.
1856 Her daughter Gisela is born on 15 July.
In autumn the royal couple with their daughter Sophia visit Venice, passing through Laibach and Trieste.
1857 Journey to northern Italy.
The empress suffers from psychological problems. In May she journeys to Hungary with her two daughters, who both fall ill. Sophia dies in Budapest on 29 May.
1858 21 August: the crown prince Rudolph is born in Laxenburg.
1859 War in northern Italy. Elisabeth's state of health deteriorates while her husband is away at the scene of the Italian war.
She frequently goes riding and starts to practise horsejumping.
1860 The imperial couple's marriage enters a crisis.
"Escape to Madeira", almost two years' absence from Vienna.
1862 The empress's return in August is celebrated with a torchlit procession as far as Schönbrunn.
1863 Fanny Angerer (later Fanny Feifalik) becomes Elisabeth's hairdresser. It is the period of braided hairstyles; as Fanny Angerer combs the empress's hair, Elisabeth learns Hungarian.
1864 Winterhalter, an artist at the courts of Paris and London, paints portraits of the emperor and empress.
These famous paintings show Elisabeth at the height of her beauty. In November Ida Ferenczy is appointed "Her Majesty's tutor". He wins the empress's trust and an intimate friendship develops between them.
1865 Official inauguration of the Ringstrasse in the empress's presence.
Elisabeth ensures that the crown prince Rudolph receives a liberal education.
1866 Franz Joseph and Elisabeth make a journey to Hungary lasting several weeks.
The empress meets Gyula Andrássy and Ferenc Deák and increasingly lends her support to the Hungarian cause.
1867 8 June: coronation of Franz Joseph and Elisabeth in Buda.
19 June: the emperor Maximilian of Mexico is killed at Querétaro.
In August Franz Joseph and Elisabeth meet Napoleon III and Eugenie of France in Salzburg ("beauty contest between the two empresses").
1868 22 April: Elisabeth's daughter Maria Valeria is born in Budapest.
1869 Elisabeth spends almost six months on Lake Starnberg.
In December, returning from her journey to the East, Elisabeth meets the emperor at Miramare, and goes with him to Rome, where she attends the opening of the Council.
1870 Elisabeth takes part in a great hunt in the Roman countryside.
War between Prussia and France. Napoleon III is deposed; Italy conquers papal Rome.

Four-pannelled screen with numerous lithographs and engravings showing portraits of the emperor and empress and scenes from their life. Bundesmobiliendepot.

1871 From March to June and in autumn Elisabeth is at Merano, with short stays in Vienna and Ofen. Count Andrássy is appointed imperial foreign minister. By this time the persons closest to the empress are all Hungarians: the new lady-in-waiting countess Marie Festetics, Ida Ferenczy and the new first majordomo Franz von Nopcsa.
1872 At the beginning of April engagement of Elisabeth's daughter Gisela with prince Leopold of Bavaria at Ofen.
In May death of her mother-in-law, the archduchess Sophia.
1873 Universal exhibition in Vienna: the crown prince Frederick William of Prussia, king Leopold of Belgium, tsar Alexander II, the heir to the English throne Prince Edward, the German empress Augusta, the queen of Spain Isabella and the shah of Persia visit Vienna. Crash of the Stock Exchange. Threat of cholera in Vienna.
1874 In January Elisabeth is in Munich with Gisela, who has given birth to her first child.
With King Ludwig of Bavaria the empress feels a spiritual affinity, though it becomes increasingly difficult for her to see him. In Munich she visits a hospital for cholera victims and a lunatic asylum.
Franz Joseph journeys to Russia.
The empress amuses herself by dressing up as the yellow domino "Gabriel" at the Carnival ball in the great hall of the musical Society.
Late July: Elisabeth's first journey to England, together with Maria Valeria.
1875 The emperor Ferdinand I, who had abdicated in 1848, dies in Prague. Franz Joseph is his sole heir. From her husband's bequest Elisabeth receives two million florins.
1876 At the end of January Ferenc Deák dies, deeply mourned by Elisabeth. In England Elisabeth devotes herself almost exclusively to exhausting and dangerous hunts on horseback; under the guidance of Bay Middleton, one of the best riders in England, she is celebrated as the "queen behind the horse team". In September she visits Corfu. During the hunts on horseback at Gödöllö she again sees Bay Middleton.
1877 The empress's niece Marie Wallersee is engaged to be married to count Georg Larisch. The crown prince also takes part in the hunts at Gödöllö.
1878 The empress participates in hunts in Northamptonshire, again under the guidance of Bay Middleton.
Rumours about Elisabeth and Middleton cause tensions with Rudolph.
1879 At the beginning of January Elisabeth attends the court ball; her charm and beauty are unaltered.
April: the imperial couple celebrate their silver wedding anniversary, a parade of the city of Vienna pays tribute to them along the Ringstrasse.
1880 Journey to England.
1881 Another visit to England where Elisabeth stays at the castle of Lord Combermere in Cheshire. Bay Middleton guides her for the last time in the horseriding hunts.
10 May: marriage of the crown prince with Stephanie of Belgium.
In September King Umberto of Italy and Queen Margherita visit Vienna.
8 December: fire in the Ringtheatre in Vienna; all the scheduled hunts are suspended.
1882 Another journey to England.
At the spring parade in Vienna Elisabeth appears on horseback in all her magnificence.
Building work is begun on the Villa of Hermes in the park of Lainz.
1883 September: the crown prince's daughter, Elisabeth, is born in Laxenburg.
November: Katharina Schratt acts for the first time at the court

theatre of Vienna and becomes the emperor's favourite actress.
1884 Visit of Queen Elisabeth of Rumania, who writes with the pseudonym "Carmen Sylva". She had become a model much-admired by Elisabeth, whose literary ambitions are confirmed by the visit of her "poetess colleague".
1885 Elisabeth enthusiastically studies the works of Homer. October: great journey to the East on the yacht "Miramar", stopping off at Lacroma and Corfu, Patras, Corinth and Zante, as far as the strait of the Dardanelles, from where she visits Troy; she then proceeds to Smyrna, Rhodes, Cyprus, Port Said and Alexandria, and, passing through Ithaca, returns to Corfu. She is accompanied by the Austrian consul in Corfu, Alexander von Warsberg, one of the greatest contemporary experts on Greece.
1886 Completion of the Villa of Hermes in the park of Lainz. King Ludwig II dies in Lake Starnberg.
1887 All year Elisabeth journeys restlessly through Europe: she stays at the spa of Temesvar, visits Carmen Sylva in Rumania, goes to Germany and England, and in the autumn travels in the Mediterranean, to Albania, Ithaca and Corfu.
1888 Elisabeth studies ancient and modern Greece with professor Romanos. Alexander von Warsberg is commissioned to build a palace on the island of Corfu.
In November Elisabeth's father, Duke Max, dies.
24 December: on the day of the empress's 51st birthday Maria Valeria celebrates her engagement to archduke Francesco Salvator.
1889 30 January: tragedy of Mayerling. At dawn the corpses of the crown prince and his lover, baroness Mary Vetsera, are discovered. Elisabeth, the first to be informed, undertakes to break the news to the emperor. Elisabeth is assailed by a profound melancholy.
Spiritistic tendencies of the empress, who attempts to enter into contact with her dead son.
In winter she travels to Sicily, Malta and Tunis and visits the ruins of Carthage.
Elisabeth gives away all her light-coloured clothes; from this time on she wears only dark-coloured garments.
Christmas is spent at Miramare, without a tree and without the traditional distribution of gifts.
1890 February: death of count Andrássy; the empress visits his widow in Budapest.
On 31 August the wedding of Maria Valeria with Francesco Salvator. For the empress this means being separated from the person dearest to her, therefore another stroke of ill fortune. Nothing links her to her home any more. England, Portugal, Gibraltar, Tangiers, Oran, Algiers, Corsica, the French Riviera, Florence, Pompeii, Capri, are the stops on a months-long journey which ends at Corfu, where Elisabeth stays for only a few days to see the progress on the construction of her palace.
1891 Journey to Greece and Sicily.
In autumn the palace known as the "Achilleion" is completed.

From Corfu she visits Egypt.
By this time Elisabeth has also learnt modern Greek. Her teacher is the Macedonian scholar Constantine Christomanos.
1892 Death of Elisabeth's mother, the duchess Ludovica.
The empress spends spring at Corfu.
At Gödöllö the hunting stables, having fallen into disuse, are dismantled.
1893 Passing through Majorca, Elisabeth visits Barcelona, then the Riviera and from there goes to Geneva and Territet; in March visit of Franz Joseph. After the emperor's departure, Elisabeth resumes her travels: Lake Como, Milan, Genoa and Naples. In a letter, the empress confesses to her husband that she would like to sell the Achilleion; she is in fact more reluctant than ever to become attached to a place.
1894 At Alicante Elisabeth meets archduke Louis Salvator, a globetrotter like herself and a man of informal manners.
Later, at Cap Martin (French Riviera) she visits the former empress Eugenie.
In the autumn Elisabeth journeys to Algiers.
1895 In mid-January Elisabeth returns from Algiers to Cap Martin. The empress is fasting more rigidly than ever.
Journey to Corsica and Corfu. After having had a monument to the crown prince Rudolph erected at the Achilleion, the empress goes to Venice, the once Austrian city, where she visits the Italian royal family.
1896 Passing through Cannes, Naples, Sorrento and Corfu, at the end of April Elisabeth visits Budapest to take part in the festivities celebrating the thousand years of the Hungarian state. At the beginning of May, together with Franz Joseph, she inaugurates the exhibition of the millenium. On the occasion of these ceremonies the Hungarians welcome their queen with frenzied ovations.
At Schönbrunn the empress goes on numerous excursions and walks with Frau Schratt.
1897 Elisabeth is nervous, pessimistic and in despair. At Territet, on Lake Geneva, she meets the heir to the throne, Franz Ferdinand. His personal doctor Viktor Eisenmenger discovers symptoms of oedema caused by hunger.
1898 March: sojourn at Territet, her partner in Greek conversation is Frederic Barker. At the end of April she meets Franz Joseph at Kissingen, and in May Maria Valeria comes to visit.
In the summer, at Ischl, the empress meets her husband and Maria Valeria for the last time.
In mid-July she goes to Bad Nauheim by way of Munich, and then, together with Barker and countess Sztáray, returns to Lake Geneva passing through Mannheim, Homburg and Frankfurt.
On 10 September she is stabbed to death by the Italian anarchist Luigi Lucheni, and on 17 September is buried in the crypt of the Capuchins.

The empress's apartment was reached by her, and by most visitors, through the Great Atrium, which was reached from the stairway of the eagles. In the small atrium today, the porter's room, stands a life-size statue of Elisabeth, executed by Hermann Klotz in 1906 as a design for the monument to the unforgettable empress. The furnishings of this large room take us back to the 18th century. In the fine rococo pannelling are paintings representing the children of the empress Maria Theresa during a performance.

ELISABETH'S GENEALOGICAL TREE

- Frederick, count palatine of Zweibrücken (1724-1726)
  - Maria Frances of Sulzbach
  - Maximilian I. Joseph (1756-1825)
    1795 duke of the Palatinate-Zweibrücken
    1799 prince elector
    1805 king of Bavaria
    - Augusta Wilhelmina Maria of Hesse-Darmstadt
    - Caroline of Baden
    - Ludwig I (1786-1868) king of Bavaria 1825-1848
      - Theresa of Saxe-Hildburghausen
      - Maximilian II (1811-1864) king of Bavaria
        - Maria of Prussia
        - Ludwig II (1845-1886) king of Bavaria
        - Otto (1848-1916) king of Bavaria
      - Otto (1815-1867) king of Greece
      - Luitpold (1821-1912) prince regent of Bavaria
        - Augusta princess of Tuscany
        - Ludwig III (1845-1921) king of Bavaria
        - Leopold (1846-1930)
          - Gisela archduchess of Austria
    - Augusta (1788-1851)
      - Eugénie Beauharnais
    - Elisabeth (1801-1873)
      - Frederick William IV king of Prussia
    - Sophia (1805-1872)
    - Ludovica (1808-1892) - - - Maximilian
  - Maria Anna (1753-1824) - - - William, count palatine of Birkenfeld-Gelnhausen (1752-1837), 1765 first duke in Bavaria
    - Maria Anna, countess palatine of Zweibrücken-Birkenfeld

- Pius Augustus, duke in Bavaria (1786-1837)
  - Louisa Amelia of Arenberg

- Maximilian (1808-1888) duke in Bavaria
  - Ludovica of Bavaria
  - Ludwig (1831-1920) duke of Bavaria
    - Henrietta baroness of Wallersee
  - Helena (1834-1890)
    - Maximilian of Thurn and Taxis
  - Elisabeth (1837-1898)
    - Franz Joseph (1830-1916) emperor of Austria king of Hungary
    - Sophia (1855-1857)
    - Gisela (1856-1932)
      - Leopold of Bavaria
    - Rudolph (1858-1889)
      - Stephanie of Belgium
      - Elisabeth (1883-1963)
        - Otto of Windischgrätz
    - Maria Valeria (1868-1924)
      - Francesco Salvator
  - Karl Theodor (1839-1909)
    - Sophia of Saxony
  - Maria (1841-1925)
    - Francesco II king of the Two Sicilies
  - Mathilde (1843-1925)
    - Louis of Bourbon, count of Trani
  - Sophia (1847-1897)
    - Ferdinand of Orléans, duke of Alençon
  - Maximilian Emanuel (1849-1893)
    - Amalia of Saxe-Coburg-Gotha